INBETWEENLAND

Jacks McNamara

INBETWEENLAND

Jacks McNamara

Deviant Type Press
OAKLAND, CA

Published by Deviant Type Press
www.devianttype.net

Published in the United States of America

Printed in Oakland, CA on 100% recycled pcw stocks

ISBN 978-0-9820159-6-4

Second Deviant Type Printing 2014

Cover Design: Gold Dust Studio
Cover Image: Voula O'Grady
Book Design: Jacks McNamara

All Paintings by Jacks McNamara

Contents

3 • The Things No One Told You About Angels

4 • Towards Fire

For all the Icaristas, and especially Sascha

PART ONE

The City With a Lake for a Heart

Diaspora

Another extinguished morning
bits of ash and discarded blossoms
empty bed and an empty page
the old hunger for witnesses.

I wake from dreams of lost
family–the one I was trying to build
with a beautiful woman who did not laugh
at my jokes, and the family who kicked me out
of the wooded Virginia hills
for being queer and crazy
I never could tell which
or the difference–but now
I find myself in a paved and distant valley
crusted with houses and filled with queers
from other landscapes, I find
myself tasting the word diaspora
wondering if I am allowed it
since we did not belong where we began –
settlers on stolen land.

I scan front yards daily
for Angel's Trumpets
and other poisonous miracles
scan my corner nightly
for another gunshot body and I wish
I could go home
if I knew where it was.

Only the hills at high noon
rising over the freeway
remind me I am standing
on the same Earth.

The Archaeology of Snow

1

I remember the way the Western sun
would light up the negative spaces
between the leaves of the very first house plant
I ever managed to keep alive
in the first place that felt like a home.
My bedroom window faced 10,000 other houses
stacked up on the hill that kept back the fog,
San Francisco afternoons creating space to stop
leaving for the first time in 22 years.
I learned to paint lichens, lightning, and candles.
Wings with taproots.
Rivers the color of bruise. Inevitably
one housemate got pregnant and rented
a tiny apartment with the boy downstairs.
Another moved back to Texas and I
gave everything away
moved into the bed of my truck.

2

California has too many freeways
and never enough snow.
The long summer of 2005 was broken by fantasies
of winter, exploded roses on my skin,
and the beginning of seizures
when overexposed filmstills from 1985
began to erupt out of my sacrum.
The psychic called it kundalini rising.
The homeopath gave me snake venom.
The psychiatrist called me a liability
and dropped me because I was a suicide risk.
When I visited back east I drank wine in the morning
slept with my best friend's girlfriend
could eat nothing but fried chicken for days.
When I returned to California
I could not find the light switches

in my room. I spent mornings drawing birds
on telephone wires, instead of going to work.
When the fog closed over August
I decided to move to apple country
in mid-October, when the leaves would be full of flames.

3

After apple country froze solid and thawed
slowly, my mother down south began to die.
She did not do it gracefully. Her organs failed
on a Sunday, while I was milking a goat.
Come home now. Board the train
back to a state saturated with corporate
headquarters where there used to be horse pastures,
a damp yard where the garage smells like a hospital
and mothers are filled with stale blood.
Attached to machines while their feet turn black
and their bellies swell with the sepsis
that looks like lost children. I become certain
her last words are a bitter critique of my haircut
until she rises from the nearly dead and glows
through cheeks her favorite shade of fuchsia,
eating nothing but canned peaches and cottage cheese
for 6 weeks, sitting up until summer is starving the crops
and she lays back down.

I find myself holding her hand
while she suffocates to death in the living room
where she used to drink cheap wine.
She leaves us to withstand
the next year's blizzards alone.

4

California was a relief again after all that snow.
The misplaced palm trees, the flat anonymous sun,
the queers dressing their dogs in hooded sweatshirts.
You could get lost with the anarchists
eating 30 pounds of dumpstered chocolate
in a warehouse with boards over the windows

or become invisible with the Buddhists
facing walls or stripping paint
in silence. In the used bookstore on 16th
where the peacefountain by the register
bubbled loud enough to drown
out the neighboring taqueria and the SRO
the owner, a complete stranger, handed me
100 sheets of crumpled Rumi
to keep me company until 8:37 am
when the daily mariachi music
drifted up through the floorboards of my room
from the dollar store downstairs. In that bookshop
I found the volume of poetry that broke
my voice open again, and showed me
how to write down the unrelenting itch
and ache of exile in crowded land, the sugar
in the vortex of a passionflower, the sound
of the dead with their heavy feet
pacing the roof upstairs
keeping me awake all night.

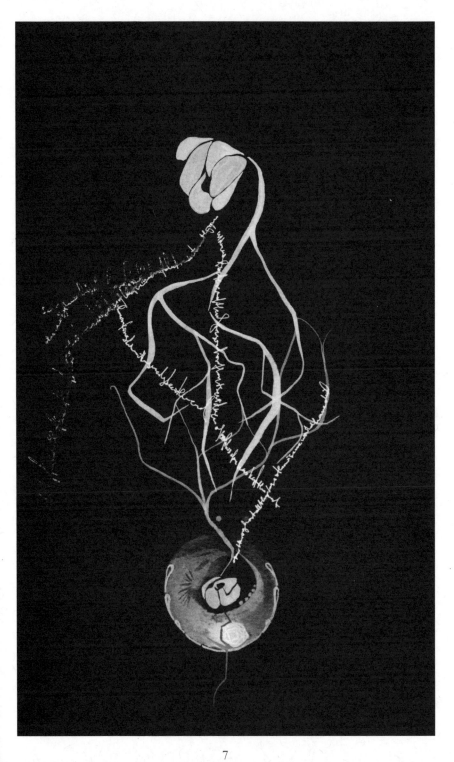

The City of Reluctant Blooms

It must be enough to kill me
this time. Except
it's not. Somehow I ride
through the night air
my bike
home. There is chocolate cake
a broken shower. One
leaking candle & a dream
so strong it wakes a woman
who phones across an ocean
to make sure I'm still alive.

I am. I ask
about our dog. I ask
about our house. I spill
a vase of pomegranate stems
across a painting in progress
and swear. Memory –
fuck memory.   *white chalk*
cliffs above the ancient
English sea   we almost
throw our rings over the edge   we have one
last night in the back of the van
apricot sun over the moving truck
longest dusk.
                                    Now
an orchid has opened in Oakland
here, in my room. I
will have to stick around
to keep it watered.

Piano

Some mornings come
I am reading about psychotherapy
and lightning. My room so bright
when the wall outside my window
reflects the early sun. Until
sudden rain pours
on the sagging balcony
and its rotting carpet, pours
on all the crabgrass and shining
streets.

Some mornings are blocked
and nearly broken, her locked
door, his swollen eyes, the lure
of computers and too much bread.
I check on the penstemon blossoms
out back, visit
the dew.

Some mornings are tendrilled
and expectant. Love letters
that never come. One more question
about the future. Leftover lentils
and smoke. I know this whispering music
like rib songs, like cicada fire,
like nearly. there. the small blades
of spring. Under my fingernails
someone else's cells. An eyelash
waiting for a wish. Piano keys
I am just relearning to play.

So Many Ways to Be Beautiful

this is a story about when your mom died and a boy loved you and a boy
left you and a girl
loved you and you left her and your dad left too.
this is a story about the neighborhood with singed wings and pride
like a barbecue smoking out back.
this is a story about not giving up over and over again.
this is a story about believing you have a broken heart
not a mental illness.
this is a story about the ache you come home to every night
and learn to hold in your arms like the child you once were
even though no one held you in their arms back then.
this is a story about becoming capable of leaving enough space
between words
that someone else can read your story too.
this is a story about learning
to cook squash
cut hair
connect pipes
drive stick
mix flesh tones
lay down loops
fix your brakes
grow garlic
get consent
and take no prisoners.
this is a story about bleeding a poem wearing a cock making a skirt hiding
your shame knotting a tie and using the heel of your boots to bring her
home.

this is a story about the end times and the way they become the beginning
if you survive the empty hours the end of June pull your mother's ring
off the shelf where it's slept with a lock of her hair since the moon went
black and light a candle know you were loved pull a song from your throat
and a stone from his lungs, remember that you are stronger than all the
nightmares ghosts and police.

this is the shape of almost but not quite. home. ok. a perfect horrible city
where brown boys get shot by white cops, where white girls cry while

helicopters fly, over and over the backyard, where babies are still learning to walk and the fog always cancels July.

shape of sound shape of sky shape of too many names for nowhere and nowhere left to hide. city of potholes city of angels city of passionflower salt and song what if

what if we finished what we started what if we brought the pigs down what if we wrote the books that no one else is writing about the lives we are still living the bodies we are still loving the signals we are crossing the men at the border the women on the street the people with mismatched pronouns and fucked up hair the people with bound breasts pink heels striped pants gender dysphoria and so many ways to be beautiful that only the schoolchildren can find the names. what if. what if we brought our gospel home.

Lemon Tree

She says it is such a pretty tree
despite the flailing limbs & giant
fruits speckled with the black grime
that condenses each night in the dew
settling on the broken chairs & stubborn
blossoms of West Oakland. She tells me

it is pretty because we are trying not
to talk about the other thing, the salt
words spilled into wounds I do
and do not see, a white person loving
a brown woman in a green silk dress,
bacon grease on the hem. She is pretty,
I am handsome, we are angry and we

are a pair eating pancakes and trying
not to fight over the lost islands and rust—
belt cities in our sentences, in
our skins. I finally agree. The tree
is pretty. Watching it sparkle
so slightly in the wind is easier
than staring at walls and eyes
gone blank. I am astonished
when she places her hand back on my thigh.

*

I wish someone had told me
about the flowers you cannot kill,
or that in healing you lose
only what has already died.
Except they would have been lying.
Sometimes you cut what is still green

but too vigorous, the black-eyed susan
vines that block all the back windows
no matter how many times you clear them
off the dirty glass. You can tell yourself

you don't need that light anyway
but you do. The kitchen is always
too dark.

*

When she fights she is all the ages
she has ever been, 19 & 36,
12 & 4 and I am shaking,
13 and waiting for the crescendo
before the tender return of hands. Later
I will remember the poem about continents
she wrote when we were falling. Africa

who remains enormous despite the distortion
in maps drawn by empire. She redraws
maps, this woman who takes 3 daily drops
from a bottle marked Witches
Bitches and Hos, whispers
change me to goddesses of destruction
and birth. She asks me to rewrite
her body, unconquered, she writes

a poem about decolonized love.

*

Now it is February. I part the unstoppable
curls of hair across her eyes. We watch
the lemon branches through the back windows
growing towards an absolutely
unshrinkable sky.

Lung Seed

It was her idea to ask about my gender.
It was my idea to lie.
To myself. For a long time. Except
it was not my idea at all.
It is the world's idea, that we should lie
to ourselves, that we should not find names
for experiences that do not fit in boxes.
It is an idea that gets inside your own story
until you think you made it up.

To try to write this still stops my breath
head threatens to detach
like an agitated balloon lifting off
a secret body. There is a terror
to being broken, and a terror
to never being known. She gave me my name
in November, when the days were filling with rain.
It lived on one side of the Bay, this name,
for a long season of heavy soil and small rooms.
In the Spring it began to bud out and scratch
the inside of my throat, a lung seed
becoming tree. A language
determined to grow.

In June I asked the world to use the name
by emailing a FAQ to 93 people.
It referenced flapjacks
famous hitchhikers
Wikipedia's take on third gender
and a dog named Jack
from young adult science fiction
who is as immune to psychotic outbreak syndrome
as I one day hope to be.

One day of euphoria
thirty days of shame
words burning visible across my chest
hunting through every gender book on Amazon

for the things that made me spend the morning crying –
"genderqueer is on the spectrum of trans" –
visualizing the ship of my body casting off
from the harbor of woman
into something uncertain
and so much more vast.
Spent the nights reading
the things that made me come
hard, imagining
a power between my legs I had never
let myself own. Too much
to speak, almost enough
to sing. Words became brittle

words took on a shine, words
hung suspended between notes
like raindrops on cobwebs
like small bits of fabric
caught in barbed wire fence. Everything
is now open for investigation.
Shoes, hats, hours, pronouns
years. Sweating belly
hiding breasts. Too few names for nowhere
and nowhere left to rest. A city with a lake
for a heart, a summer with fog
for breath. We place our bodies
behind microphones, we place our bodies
on streets. Our bodies become words
cast off from land
navigating silver
legible at the edge of day
glitter and the dark
unknowing. We are the sounds
of sex and birdcalls the shape
of scars and clothing
piled in corners, abandoned, redrawn, we are
eyes opened in the morning
to angelbones stacked up
against a window, silhouette of change
outlined somewhere between war and the future.

PART TWO

Inbetweenland

Whether or Not You Fly

When I grow up I wanna be Brandi Carlile
I wanna sing to tear the roofs off houses
and serve you up your own heart on a plate.
When I grow up, I just wanna feel at home
in this boygirl body, at home on 10,000
foot mountains, at home
in my own bed. I wanna navigate
rush-hour traffic with regular breath, get along
with my family, make love
with my eyes wide open
and call down the rain when I come. When I grow up
I wanna jump off every waterfall
without ever having to flinch.

I love you even if you can't jump
even if you stand at the top of the cliff shaking
wishing for your mom
even though she was so cruel. I love you
in those moments when you can't speak
move, sing, jerk off, or smile. Those moments
when you need to be small again –
small and held, not small and brave.
I love you in those moments when you compare
your hair to every other girl, your muscles
to every other boy, when you look
around the room and find yourself deficient
because that is what you were trained to find.
I love you with sand in your underwear
after a wave knocks you out, I love you trying
to pee when no one's looking, I love you unwitnessed
hungry, lonely, and done. I witness you.

I witness you talking to that beat up 11 year old girl
inside your own chest, the one who can't believe
someone's finally listening to her. I witness you bring her glitter,
ice cream, and daisy chains, I witness you describing
the perfect getaway that never happened
how all your friends would come bust her out of the house & fly

through the sky in a blue car like Harry Potter
and land somewhere safe.
Safe.
Later, I witness you hiking alone
12 miles up and down ridges in the rain
and the sun, anchoring your heels into earth
your lungs to the sky, becoming part
of the widest expanse of ocean you have ever seen.
I witness you hitching the last ride down the mountain
to the last plate of fried chicken
in the last town at the edge
of the colonized world. I watch you wake up the next day
pray to the sunrise
press flowers in a book
for your girl back home. I witness you navigating
potholes, dehydration, Easter Sunday, and unrelenting wind.
I witness you wanting a family so bad you could taste it.
I witness you hoping
this girl is the one. Hoping one day
you get to plant the blueberry bushes
you're both keeping in pots
cause you're waiting for them to root in the ground
together. I witness you calculating
budgets, debating careers, trying to paint, love, fuck
and make poems despite all the anxiety
of hustling a life under capitalism.

You are doing such a good job.

You are making it, you adult, you dreamer, you kid.

I see you when you count to three
and leap in the sky shrieking
only to find when you land
the water is actually deep enough to hold you.

Mornings After

This morning everything, even the handkerchief,
smells like bitter herbs. I wish my hand would grow
skin over the bare places where her car, *The Love-Muscle,*
bit me while I bit her. The book
for survivors reassures me: *even if*
you have initiated sex twice today
you can initiate it again. I am sore in the right places
and the ribs, the belly, where I am letting go of my last
lover, like the maple's skeleton dropping
red leaves in January, because winter in California
is also fall, also spring. My new lover lets me open her
with fingers and fists. Her eyes are inbetween
brown and green, the light of dirt and seeds.
I have never seen them without their sharpness on
before. The morning after the morning of. She wears
a red dress and glitter, 36 going on 13. I cannot contain
the grin that spills from my ears and downturned eyes
too bright like the sun and the sounds of dishes
in the booth where we are, for the first time, shy.

If only a scab would form
on the ring finger of my right hand
before the plum blossoms burst again
and late rain knocks them all off the trees.

Love is a Messy Broken Thing
Part 1

The artichokes out back are blooming an iridescent purple fire like God's eyelashes reeking of honey and calling the bees and I think this time I have found the women to spin sticky dreams with this time the women who ask for my body and my singing voice this time I will paint music the inside of water the spilled intricacies of blood and how fiercely we want the promises of what begins and what will last our fingers tangled in ink or earth ready to plant ready to write ready to make mix tapes and climb mountains 14,000 feet high but I am not ready for the spiked flowers to let loose their silver parachute seeds not ready for paintings torn in half and started over not ready for never or especially *nevermind.*

Love is a Messy Broken Thing
Part 2

Love is a Messy Broken Thing
Part 3

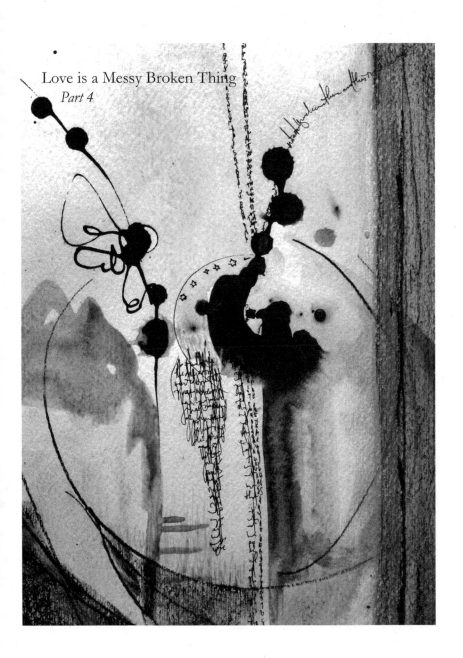

Love is a Messy Broken Thing
Part 4

Love is a Messy Broken Thing
Part 5, West Oakland

In my fingerprints
flotillas and femmes
a conspiracy of crushed colors
good intentions
dry blood. I rinse
the pigment from my skin
attempt a return
to this corner lot
where the sky is breaking
the stems of flowers
crackle like bleached bones
the sun leaks
and birds hide
in the shelter of one almost
tree, here, it is morning.

From a pitched roof
2 gulls keep watch
over the chainlink fences
sleeping guns
pale roses.
I notice the light on my feet
remember the drone of endless helicopters
think of my housemate's bruises
from a beating down the street.
I hear violins and trash trucks
smashed glass and bacon frying --
I wonder about the shape of peace.
Gulls depart. I notice the violence settling
in the creases of my skin
almost invisible
like the fine dust of late summer
that sticks to everything.

Love is a Messy Broken Thing
Part 6, 10th and Adeline

This sadness is bigger than B vitamins, it
is not interested in working around my schedule, or
all your good ideas, it arrives anyway
on wings of fog and stays a while
like the houseguest you didn't invite
but she does the dishes so
you don't kick her out.

There was this church, you see,
with crumbling steps that held us
while we sat under a sun
with all its gentle burned out.
Her eyes shone like an oil slick.
I could not stop touching her thigh.
She told me about this casualty of war
called her heart, which did not have permission
to fall in love with me right now.
I peeled paint and relocated my gaze
to the strangled trees at the edge of the parking lot
where something called never was stealing my breath.

Yesterday I found this same church in a dumpster
bigger than my house, its ribs splintered
across the sky and reeking, its borders patrolled
by men in enormous machines
with no sense of our shared history.

April

You are sure you don't belong on this planet. All the sinister creatures, the wind with teeth. The bloodgold trees are made more of memory than of leaves today, this bed made more of unfinished songs than sheets. Your burnt tongue seems evidence of having lived on Earth. Somewhere you watched a woman die. You failed to return a phone call. You fell in love with a dangerous head of curls. At least the birds are unequivocal. Ravens the size of turkeys, turkeys as big as trees, scraping their tails loudly across the beat down track like a snowplow or a cardboard box. Longer skies are returning to April and with them promises of overly ripe fruit, promises of cruelty, snapped off peas, and all the ghosts you failed to save. Every month has its tragedy. April has two.

It Has a Ragged Blue Edge

Headlights reflected off concrete walls, concrete walls sprouting those trees that take 2 months to turn red. The sadness has soft hair, combed across the sky like end of day clouds. It sounds like the birds heading north and the trucks heading west. It settles like more sleep into the mattress, and tastes slightly like rain. I imagine it disappearing down the grate like the almost–rainbows of oil mixed with melted snow. I can only seem to love it when no one else is around.

In the afternoon space where a mother is alone in a shadowy room waiting for her child to get home from school, it spreads. She has time to remember the things she never told anyone before she became a mother. Maybe she will tell them to her child while they eat a snack. Maybe her child will find her on the floor, face down in the carpet, not sure why it is worth getting up anymore. Maybe that will happen years later, after the child leaves the house and starts painting her fingernails blue, wearing old clothes from the dollar-a-pound store. In the city with subway tokens and small diners where she will buy grilled cheese sandwiches with the friend who got kicked out of school. Maybe they will stay up all night, until 9 AM, and she will kiss the boy with fish lips and know it's not worth kissing boys after all. She will send him home when the daylight turns that color like the end of a cigarette. She will slide under stiff sheets and feel her hair wrapped like a soft scarf around her neck for one of the last times. When she wakes up, the streetlamps will be turning on.

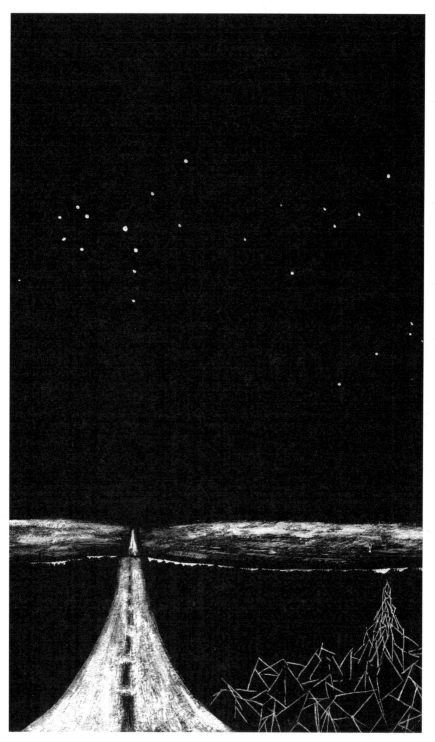

31

Lovesong For Mama

I can only seem to grieve for you in my dreams
when things happen that should not happen –
my father appears with a woman groomed and coached
to look exactly like you, back when you could walk,
and tells me to call her Kim, which was your name,
even though she is young, blonde, and obedient
which you were not.
I start screaming like a child in a war zone
to make sure everyone knows
that my mother is dead.
I bawl hysterically and run
down the halls of some dark mansion,
collapsing in a stranger's bed. When morning comes,
in the dream, I expect a man who hugs and terrifies me
to kiss my cheek and try to know my mind.
Instead they have brought a doctor
enclosed my wrist in a plastic band
marked with the first date I was held down
by three nurses and given a shot
for my own good. I was three.
Now I am not allowed to speak.

When I wake in the raw pink dawn of the real world
my eyes are burning. Through the kitchen window
the land is frozen solid and it glows.
I check for a message from a woman who loves me
which you would hate, because she is a woman.
I light the stove and remember
you were the first woman who broke my heart.
I was told, over and over, that you loved me
by my father, who could not make you stop.
Even if I could not see it
this was love: contempt, rage, hysteria, despair.
Clearly love was a painful thing, or it did not exist at all.
Love could not be demonstrated, it could only be described
like Santa Claus or Cinderella. Love did not feed you
or touch you, or learn who you were becoming.
Love required excuses and objections. It required a defense.

Love could not be felt, or seen; it was invisible
like death, or the future.

I had other ideas. This was wrong.
Life was supposed to be different. It should be fair
and somewhat rational. There should be rules
and predictable outcomes. Hungry people
should be fed, sad people
should be held, rich people
should be generous, all people
should be free. Clearly, I was crazy.
Clearly, I did not understand the way things work.

When you died, perfect, of gangrene and booze
you taught me that the world is sick and needs healers.
You never even had to say the words.

Why Bodhisattvas Stare at Walls

The old winter light like the desert.
The memory of war in green places. The dryness
in our mouths, the paralysis in our limbs, the way it feels
to let your skull be heavy against the floor, the rising
and falling, the walk we should be taking
to end the word *should*, the way it all wells up
between our ears; the songs, the grief, the attempts
to keep the sun on our skin for a thousand years,
to balance at the edge of a ruined hill,
to stand under the planets when the night is so cold
breathe through our bellies in the dark
and look up. To be full of horizon when the wind is gray
and there is no grave to visit, to yell at the rain, to wake up
anyway, be kissed anyway, chop onions
fold clothes, talk to angels, and sit still
even though he is leaving, even though she is gone, even though
we are coughing and parched and the ending
is unclear, even though the empty hours are coming –
the empty hours are here. Her hair is in a silver box.
The morning glory died. The cactus downstairs
has small pink flowers
that bloom like stars in November
on broken arms covered in spikes.

Sea Glass

She wishes you dreams like honey
but you wake from dreams like salt
on wounds you are busy forgetting
while you work for the white man all day.

You pick fights with yourself now
because you can't stand losing other people
anymore. Loss has made you hard
and handled you smooth like ocean
handles sea glass, nickel or knife.

& there were hallelujahs on the radio at night

A poem arrives on the wings of a mosquito
to wake you up, burns
your knuckles, sets in motion
the familiar vigilance, your hands
waving, the music in the corners
of your mind swelling to dark
reds and underwater greens,
something like candles, something
like rage. Dreams of lava, dreams
of maps, trails you almost find.
An answer in your palm
pressed to clavicle, the beating
inside, you try to remember
how to feel your legs
wonder when they left
which night in the desert
which moment of shock
between your skin and the real –
stranger's hands under your zipper
wake you into striking
4 a.m. in Egypt
nowhere left to go. Departure
the flat stretch of empty
beside an empty road
where only you could hear the notes
of an early future chorus.

Too Bright To See

This cannot be spoken.
It lives in the spine
it closes the throat it escapes
through the hips leaping and twitching
with the electric shock of what absolutely cannot be spoken.
As the colors begin to erupt from between the blades of her shoulders
she exists in the walls, she retreats to the shaft of light
on the southwest side of the room she is deep in the plant
struggling towards the window but she does not inhabit her body and she
does not exist in the words that have vanished like water into ice.
It is colder than fire it is louder than wind, this silence
this absence
behind her eyes pressed closed
so hard because no one
no one can see her now.

If there were a word it would be shame
but this is not a word it is a meteorological event
it is an earthquake   it is a war.
This is too bright too blinding
5 years old   an uncle   his white shorts
Florida   the blazing   being forced
to take him in her mouth —
she cannot speak

about being forced to take it
to her lover
who is a man   who is a woman   who is
trying to resuscitate her
in a foreign country
where it is winter and it is not
1985
not Florida
soft skin   urgent voice
do you know where you are
do you know who you are
(Someone has swallowed her words
far back in the screaming silence.)

She becomes smaller and curls
into the black. The convulsions
rip through like aftershocks
tears stream and finally
she opens her eyes.

Born. Again. To another stranger
begging, *do you know who I am?*
Mess. Mucus
everywhere. Sheets
tangled. The weather
confusing. The hour
uncertain. The day
gone or is it just beginning?
The walls are brighter than the eyes
of her lover
distressed
blue. Her eyes are
blue   the man's were
brown   the man had
a beard in the heat
and a laugh too big
for the secrets she had to keep.

Sunflower

In the mornings, she made her bed, made her breakfast, and packed her lunch. She was 6. In the evenings, she listened. To you. For hours. Until you would collapse on the kitchen floor, sobbing, and your husband would carry you upstairs. Then she made dinner, studied, and talked to her own reflection in a tiled wall. She was 11. She didn't tell the neighbors.

You made her iron her shorts. And yours. You told her she looked like a streetwalker when she showed up in a dress that was covered in sunflowers, but too wide, because she was too skinny, because you did not feed her. Anything that she should eat.

She learned three languages anyway. She won 7 awards. She wrote plays, drew you roses, made you omelettes, and called you on your racism when you couldn't keep your mouth shut in front of the T.V. When you died, she was holding your hand.

Now she might be done. Speaking to you, speaking to your husband, calling you mother or father or ghost. It is time to heal, and healing involves telling the neighbors. Healing involves fucking women, growing flowers, being fed. Her knuckles are bruised from the things she had to punch after her father broke her heart one last time and she is done with the violence. These are the days when the world is waking up. These are the days when she is ready to be loved. You can have your silence, your rages, and your blank blank eyes. Hers are burning open.

On Returning

Bass and the rattling floors called home.
Waiting inside an old black dress
with a hole like an estuary
spreading as the tide comes in.
After too many nights
listening to the arguments of stars
instead of sleeping, your arms
are too thin to carry more dreams.

You are sure that this year
has been overtaken by Bermuda grass
aphids, and snails. Nothing more
will grow. God's many voices
have gone underground. Greece
is crashing through the center of the earth.
Re-read Baudelaire, Rimbaud, Verlaine.

Read Patti Smith. Don't stop
until the end. Stand
at the cutting board
downstairs. Sever a head
of garlic from the braids
curing on the kitchen wall.
Remember what saved your life.

If you feel the weight of the knife
certain in your hands, sing
something you still remember
until daylight savings time begins –
you might have a chance

at hope. A baby's toenail –
moon-shaped. tiny. clean.

In the morning, birds will flock music
over the parking lot. Sit on the busted wall
whose concrete keeps back the Bay. Know:
they are taking over the streets
in more cities than you can name.

Inbetweenland

I wish someone had told me I would get out of the burning house –
or that I had already escaped
a long time ago – and it lived on
only in my muscles and my mind.
I wish someone had handed me the word
survivor
placed it in my palms
like a blossom or a drill
told me to build altars and hang
hinges. Carefully. I wish
they had told me
I could stand up any time
open the door
leave.

~

It is 1986. I am lying
on my back in a hot room.
My father blocks the door
tells me fairy tales with cruel endings
Goldilocks shut in a closet and forced
to eat beetles
by her parents
after she gets lost in the woods.

He leans over to kiss me
on the lips where I don't want
to be kissed. Wishes me
good night. Again.

~

It is 2006. I am lying
on my back in a room with red velvet
curtains, walls covered
in fairies and pelts. Lying on the table
of a psychic named Sue

whose hands know things
I can't explain.

She touches my shoulders and asks where I am.

In space.

Asteroids   comets   a large
silence of almost nothing.
That far away?
No wonder I can't find you.

My eyes are closed.
I cannot tell if I am sinking or floating.
You haven't chosen
to stay on this earth yet
have you? No.
26 years and counting.

~

I wish someone had told us that the years spent journeying back and
forth across Inbetweenland would not be a waste. That the miles and
blizzards could not be avoided. That we would find the necessary roads,
the necessary words, the mystery between them both. I wish they had
told us about earthquakes. That we were not crazy. That sometimes the
unspeakable
erupts out of the fault lines
in your spine. That the body
stops shaking   the ground
stops buckling despite
aftershocks despite fire
eventually
something settles
water turns clear
birds come back in the morning
you choose earth
make breakfast
go on.

~

My best friend and I used to talk
about choosing earth and sky
we traveled between borders leading
workshops for survivors
who had known rocks that whisper
billboards who shout conspiracies
and cosmic truths, electric hearts
impaled on apocalypse sunsets
over ruined cities and paper mountains
speaking myths that evaporate
like water off hot pavement
when you finally come down

into the world of toothpaste and toilet paper
fathers and sons
appointments, diagnoses –
mania, psychosis – but we knew
we were caught trying to fly
out of the mazes built by kings and corporations
where your wings melt
once you finally make it over the sea.

. When we mentioned keeping one foot
in both worlds, everyone in the room   .
would exhale
eyes like fireflies
switching on at dusk.
Permission. This too is real.
Inbetweenland. Both. Our own maps.
You don't have to choose
between sanity and the roofless night.

~

It is 2012 and I am lying
on the floor of a small room
while a therapist in a black muscle tee
emblazoned with Hope in white letters
draws infinity symbols over my eyes.
I follow her fingers I freeze   as usual
until the images come. The shadow shapes of men

my father   leaning over   thick
stories   heat
suddenly
the impulse to roll onto my side
stand up
open the door
leave. For the first time

I do.

Outside the world is big as snow
bright as a waxing moon.
Full of people. My hands
are full of tools my eyes
full of horizon.
I am enormous.
A child landing in an adult's miraculous skin.

PART THREE

The Things No one Told You About Angels

Third Gender

1

I remember when I turned my last skirt into a tablecloth
because I only wanted to be one gender now
and it was not girl. I remember when everything changed—
I turned the tablecloth back into a skirt.

2

The red purse was the last present
my mother ever gave me. I hid it
under the bed
and then I got sober
and she went into a coma. It was easier
to look like a girl when I went back to Virginia.
The neighbors liked me with long hair.
The purse was actually pretty
and had good pockets. I carried it
to the hospital every day.

3

When I was 17 I wrote a short story
about castrating cucumbers
after cars of drunk men threw packs
of playing cards at me, queen of hearts
ace of spades, they swerved
directly at me   2 AM   screamed
at my tits. When I cut
all my hair off 2 days later
I felt hideous and proud
properly gay and partly invisible
no one screaming now but my mom.

4

They called me Sinead O'Connor
they called me G.I. Jane
they called me crazy and called me sir
when I shaved my head in a foreign country.
Small children asked if I was a boy or girl
the men shouted out shop windows
to ask where my hair was. Finally
I gave up and told them I sold it
to buy my plane ticket home.
They stopped asking why I wasn't married.
They stopped asking me anything at all.

5

We had gone to my mother's favorite restaurant
drunk enough wine to be pleasant.
We were supposed to be celebrating something.
When we got home she burst into tears
all over the kitchen counter. All she was thinking
at dinner that night was she hoped
everyone thought I'd had chemotherapy
and that's why I had no hair.

6

He told me I'd always had a lot of third gender energy
before I knew what that meant. He thought
it was a compliment. I thought
I was an alien. I don't remember
another word he said. I remember going home
putting on a black dress
and trying to be beautiful.

7

Now my lover tells me I am handsome and she tells me
I am pretty. Sometimes
I open my ribs for her.
I bought a black tuxedo vest

on eBay. It has one rhinestone button.
I will wear it. She will wear a short skirt
and a flower in her hair. She calls me
her ex-boyfriend and she calls me a zebra
she squeals when she discovers
my underwear is covered in hearts.

The Entire Earth

1

She tells me to write about the cobweb of cum stretched between our thighs. We are in a brown tent. The afternoon is sliding down the hillside. I don't know what to say but I look out at the puzzle pieces of light between the trees and think about the ways she is more like the sun than fire. Even though the sun is fire. Even when fire is blocked by the clouds.

2

The clouds roll in over this city that is not exactly a city. Someone waters the freshly planted earth where it has begun to crumble like old pots. Sirens in the grass, a day like the African daisies that close when the dusk comes. Stretched between us, a cobweb of streets. I still smell her cunt between my legs but I will not mention it. Not yet.

3

5 leaves on the blackberries. At the edge of the woods, 5 leaves, 3 leaves, I cannot remember the meaning of numbers. On the agenda for the evening, music. A cobweb of harmonies stretched between the year of ghosts and the year of water. My hands smell like the sun. She is dissatisfied with her afternoon. A sadness overtook her like drowning after she came this morning. She held me against her chest like the entire earth.

June

More brightness than the body knows how to tolerate
these days that last until 10. All that is mending
but not yet fixed, is so plain, such a fact, in this excess of light.

I cannot tell you what the medicine is before I make it.
Only that it requires the space after dreaming
and before day. Sometimes it requires birds or torn

paper, a recipe, a spell. Over time we are growing. The locks
tricked open with credit cards and paperclips. The necessary cracks
a little wider. Sun damage begins to show. Deltas

opening from the corners of my eyes, the evidence
of what has rushed through and what continues
to overflow. The wars inside my fists are quieter, the wars

outside my room are louder, this city, this continent, I
cannot let go of the thin sound of suffering
behind the last hours of pink in the clouds.

Bruises

Sometimes when you are trying to forgive the world for its cruelty the only place you can find beauty is in the luminous red and green of stoplights, the fountains of feather grass growing out of concrete. As you bike home your neighborhood's air smells like sewage and chlorine, the front yards have been paved over, the streets are wide enough for more cars than have ever filled them, and you find yourself thinking about half–healed bruises, and trying to imagine what it would be like for them to be whole–healed. Would the soul be blank then like skin after blisters, blank but something shows, some radiant scar tissue, slightly more beautiful than bare? Is this art itself the scar tissue, does the body extend beyond borders into these pages, breathing to the soundtrack of underwater music and a percussion like wooden stars?

How to Identify Plants

You don't have to remember the names
of people. Immerse yourself in pattern language
not faces. Imagine how they survive
so many months without rain
their vertical leaves, white powders, fine hairs
spikes   rinds   roots
30 feet deep to tap groundwater
though the plant is only 6 inches high.
They are your friends and your ancestors.
They can teach you what it means to stay
and what it means to let the year change
your blossoms into the brown rattling
of seeds and fallen stalks.
They will rarely be unkind to you.
They will never remember your name.
They will offer beauty and poison
whether or not you behave.
When you cannot find the words to tell anyone
what galaxy you are hiding in
they will still be trustable, even radiant
under streetlights, without a moon.

Winter Daisies

Last night no sirens   birdcalls in our palm trees.
I harvested a perfect ear of corn
by streetlamp   by chain-link fence   by the road
where three people were shot in three weeks.
I search for revolving red lights
every night after 10.
I pack my life into boxes.
But this morning the giant elephant
trunk of the oak tree
in the park across the street   has turned green
with lichens returning in the rain around my feet
the landed flocks of geese   early light
dense grass   Oakland   your winter daisies
your skyline hovers   just a ghost.

Raining

A stranger points at the sky and says follow my finger
as he traces N O W
against the blue after the rain.
"what does it mean
for that to be a word?"

The ginkgo tree turns yellow as a crayon
in December   on the sidewalk
    of this holy city
where Decembers   are not December.

Can you hold me?
                    over the phone
                              my cheek
is against her cheek
    except it's not.

A woman on a table tells me
there are metal bars across her back
    outside the winter fields   flooded green.
She tells me black smoke
                    is on the heart side of her body
                        I pump my hands
                        into her exhaling chest
                        provide arms that she can kick
her legs into   until the black becomes
clear   the grief   raining.

Afternoon

A baseline worn out like an old sneaker
repeats through the window next to the scent
of an overblown rose and that bird with the mouth
who doesn't stop. On my wall the pinned angel
has wings like clotheslines strung with small
flags, catching wind, playing scales.

The Things No One Told You About Angels

When the sky is an oil spill
sharp moon
you always forget.

At dusk someone gives you a bicycle
and tells you the war never ends.
There is no other point. You sing loudly
all the way home.

Over the road, plain stars.
The breeze brings a ghost of long hair
across your bare neck.

You remember the night she died.
Shadows pass over your hands
you cannot keep them clean.

When you forget why we bother
doing this at all, you must find the words
for the beloved. Angels might be hearsay.
We keep each other alive.

PART FOUR

Towards Fire

What Fire Leaves Behind

I rarely speak of the wrinkles you became
at the bottom of the sea, or how I learned –

after your body poured
through my fingers

ash the exact texture
of sand where I stood –

our breath is only borrowed from the earth.

Cold Water
for David

Two Saturdays ago we descended
deep into a valley blank with fog
white and damp in the middle of summer.
I had not seen you in years; your eyes
were strangely unfocused, blue vacant
earliest morning. We took our seats. The teachers
smiled generously. We were going to practice
Transforming Anxiety and Depression now.
We were going to follow our breath
the humid space beneath a nose, the belly
rising, practice noting
the pain under the atrophied
wing muscles in our backs, all the stories
crowding for space, each
thought tipping the lever
ball runs down the obstacle course
of mind, feeling arises, body demands
we run or scream, we hold on to the life raft
of the cushion, try not to believe
those thoughts again, try to keep hold
of some choices.

You tried. You sat in an uncomfortable chair
very still, as monks who have spent many silent years
can do. Then you raised your hand, face
empty like a small child. "What if...
what if you can't feel your breath? At all
anymore? What if
you can't feel anything?" You struck me
as transparent then, a 46 year old man
made of rice paper, and frozen wind.

Later the sun burned through the trees. We walked
outside, smelled lavender blooming, picked
wild plums. Inside, the teachers gave us small blank sheets.
"This is your anti-depressant activity prescription capsule."
We congregated in groups of three

to write down the things we could do
to feel better. You were in my group.
After 10 minutes my page was full of music,
dancing, food, gardens, writing, intimacy, breath
and cold water. Your page was white. You could not remember
a single thing.
                           "Cold water?" you asked, your forehead
twisted and vague. I told you a story
about taking off all my clothes under a waterfall
the way the stagnation was pounded out of my body
8 summers ago. I showed you the tattoo
on my arm. Rocks creek sky falls reflection. "It's so you remember
what it feels like to be alive." You nodded, thoughtful.
"Would a cold shower work?" I nodded. That can help.
You wrote it down with a wobbling hand. *Cold Water.*
Showers. Go Outside.

At the end of the weekend I wished you luck
with the next chapter of your life. You were unemployed
you might be moving in with your family
after many years, everything
was unknown.

~

On Friday they found your body in your bedroom
at the San Francisco Zen Center. The monks accompanied you
downstairs, chanted the Enmei Jukku Kannon Gyo
for the protection of all life
over and over as your body made its way
to an ambulance. A few days later I found out
on Facebook. "The grief in the air at City Center
is palpable." A link to a blog post
about the ways you would laugh
the benji poem you once wrote
and how sometimes hearts just give out.

After the tears and the shaking, going outside.
I harvested all the garlic in my yard
buzzing, shocked slow and patient,
marveling at what is still alive.

Manual labor can settle the soul.
I learned and relearned this dirt
fact at those temples. I too lived at Tassajara,
Green Gulch, City Center. Swept floors
hosed mats, emptied trash, chopped
so many vegetables. Sat long periods of silence
getting to know what was broken
and what remained. It brought me peace
until it did not. One day
I got the job of combing the ashes
in the incense box. The fine gray sand
and smell of it reminded me
instantly of the aftermath
my mother's death by gangrene, a year
of panic and nightmares, flashbacks
too big for the container of zazen. Sometimes
we cannot find our breath to follow. Sometimes
the best thing is no longer to sit still.

~

After I laid the garlic out to dry
I wished I could bring you with me
in my newly repaired truck, through outrageous sunshine,
to pick up paintings and the luminous
reminders of why we are here. I wished I had told you
I too was suicidal once
in those small rooms at City Center. I too
was crushed when I realized that meditating,
however earnestly, was not enough
to save my life. I left
to learn how to move back into my body,
how to love, make a living, find a home. You
were facing the same steep hill. You

opted out. Now
your memory rides with me through Oakland. I bring you
to my beloved's house. She is at work. Suddenly
I find myself enamored
with the simplest expiring sunflower, all the bits
of broken mirror and torn magazine

scattered across her table, waiting to become art.
I don't care anymore if we succeed. It doesn't matter if we are great.
It matters that we remember the way rivers never stop
moving
     our bodies arched
across wet rocks, bare and shining
for one afternoon.
This too is real.
I let it live inside my guts
with all the nausea
and the relief. I leave
a bag of dirty clothes, a scrap
paper with the outline
one small heart.
I wish you had someone to draw
your own heart for now.
Cold water runs all down my spine.

On Sunday, Instead

Something in my dreams is burning. So is something in the world. I want the chance to be the candle spilling wax down its sides. But they say we must punch our timecards. And we do.

Until we don't. Until we wake in the unspecified silver of the rage after dawn. She takes me anyway. We take all morning. Come so hard the neighbor's dogs howl along and this time– this time we push the pillows away from our mouths. Love something impossible. The raspberries fruiting in February. I cannot help laughing apart the ladder in my spine. Don't Tweet this. It is not a status update. It is not porn. It is a fierce music. Sacred as the singing church next door.

Laughtergasm

I could paint it much more easily than write it, the cascade of yellow angles like a fractal flared staircase, or the asterisk of DNA, or the ascent of something light and broken into a million pieces—plum blossoms returning up to their trees, the way they lived before rain. That flock of white birds lifting off the fishbone shore of the Salton Sea to swim through a series of geometries in a blue sky like stars inventing the constellations. It is like that. The way 32 years of carefully constructed armor explodes and rises. Everything goes transparent and almost too bright to see, laughter an uncontrolled ringing of bells and surging of wind, blowing every cobweb out of the corner of every room, summoning all the lost children and burst buds to return.

The Right Words

It is the day after Christmas and I'm on my way home from a threesome. The glory in my surrendered hips is quickly being replaced by a familiar smoking shame. The winter's first snow has just begun to fall and I am driving through a raw gray world half dream half shine brick buildings softened slightly and everything obscured like my body I have floated partway out of my eyes that are suddenly a little too bright a little too focused my heart tight in its cage as I drive down Atlantic Avenue I search for the words the terrified deer in my chest needs to hear to move on and after making it too complicated it turns out to be so simple. I love you survivor body. Anxious and numb I still love you. You're doing such a good job. After enough repetitions my breath settles into my thighs and she lowers her gaze, bounds back into the woods.

Ars Poetica

The neon vernacular of being alive. The messy archive of breathing. The overlapping notes of music, lace, zebras. Garlic, oak trees, sky. Pierced by razor wire, the sun a hint of circle, the passionflower growing up the chain-link fence. A single bird against the sea. Radiance and closed curtains, the dry earth waiting for rain. We are questions, we are answers, we are words as yet unwritten–languages invented–the promises of tricksters and prophets, the laughter of children and time. What happens around a fire ring. What happens around a shrine.

We collect mornings. The grief that can only take shape in dreams. Her almost red hair, almost full kiss. The asymptote of home. What we write with a green pen, what we write with a noose. One dying collard tree. One rosebush the color of old silk. Our prayers. The love poems no one else is writing about the lives we are still living. In bodies boy–girl, bodies female, broken bodies, bodies becoming whole. In that space between war and the future. The ripped sound. The brushfire. The thin hair of a toddler, her fingerprints on cheap pieces of paper in an ink that will not stain. The breakfast we share. What it means to show up. Again. What it means to stay.

So many un-drunk cups of tea. Windows that leak the coldest air. Just before dawn. People trying to wake up. People shutting down. Banks before 9 AM. By dancing. Shutting them down with fists through glass. Gathering stories from Palestine. Stories from Greece. Stories from the 30 days before the locked ward, and stories from the 3 months after. Gathering in the heat. Detroit, West Oakland, New York. The unceasing wind in Death Valley. Sunrise over the Rio Grande. These aching ribs, this pressing out of words. Lung trees. So many songs. In the end, the question: how to sit still. How to be the eye of the hurricane, and write.

On Breaking up with My Girlfriend, My Job, and My Town

I finally said no. No for the sake of a full wingspan. No for the sake of the right disasters, for the sake of polka dots and black lace and kicked candles setting trash cans on fire. I said no. No for the sake of spring rain and fall prayers. For the sake of jealous monsters and small girls. No for the sake of doorways. Footsteps. Mud. No for the sake of covenants spelled out in glitter, for the sake of fisting and fighting and falling, no. No for the sake of Sunday mornings. For the sake of blow jobs and breath work, no. For the sake of risk. No. No for all the times I did not get to say no. No. No. No. No for the sake of yes. For the sake of the Smokey Mountains. For the sake of Shasta and her waters. No for dahlias, dicentra, dianthus. No for the sake of the devil I haven't met yet. No. For the sake of silence, no. No for the invention of words like tendercomplex, for spelling dork with a Q, for discovering the zebra-print adult onesie in my size at Target, and no for bringing it home. No for the sake of sharp knives and winter stars, and no for the sake of poetry. For the sake of my eyes. No for the sake of my heartbeat. No for the sake of yours.

Remyth: Country

1

It turns out you can hoe leeks
in a gold snakeskin skirt. Turns out
the willow's noonday shade
belongs to everyone and
you don't need semiautomatic weapons
to protect your kids. It turns out fear
is not a family value and the sun
is fierce on all of us.

2

One day we'll actually get to live
in those towns you pass
on your way into the mountains. The beautiful
towns with pitched rooves and too many gunracks
winter valleys like white glass
grape vines in August. We won't just stop for groceries –
we'll stay. Half the houses
full of our friends, freaky and glorious
but slower
here. now. enough time
to cut down the razor wire and cough up the smog
cry out the creeks forced underground
rest. and rest. and rest.

3

We won't have to take drugs
to turn off the radios in our heads, drink drugs
to get out of bed. We will sleep. Wake up.
work create love fuck and raise
fruit trees or children
if we want to, even
if we are three women and two men, or
one gender-variant unicorn
five sharks
and a star-bellied sneech.

Birds are the new stars
stars are actually visible
we will actually be visible
outside the five American cities
where we almost feel safe.

4

We will get to love without terror. Or
we will love the terror as it leaves
along with the morning light.

Towards Fire

1

I remember when I painted Grace as a place
with no people. Grace as a doorway
into the moon. Or hills rolling
out to horizon. Desert, sea,
a circle of perfect blue.

Grace the water
that held me aloft
under a sky with no skin
kind only in its emptiness
whispering, *Vast*.

2

I aspired to a slow heartbeat
in all situations.
Weightless bones
plenty of time.
I did not wear a watch or ride
in ambulances. I never burst
into tears and argued with cops.

Grace was a clean floor
before dawn, sitting in lotus
facing a wall. No late nights
nothing smoking. Just the murmur
of chants in a foreign language
I didn't even speak. 9 bows
3 bells. Grace
the space behind clouds.

3

One May I woke up red.

I was sure my soul had jumped
outside my skin, turned flat

as a shadow stitched on at the heels.

I set fires.

I flew 3000 miles
drank wine at lunch
sang ballads to weeds
seduced other people's trouble.

Eventually I wanted
messy things. A child
requiring haircuts. A lover
requiring meals. The other side
of a hard fight.

4

It took many years of dislocation
and weeping to shake the ribs,
many nights of scratching
scars, and startling
awake to remember
how women leave
and men violate
how women violate
and men leave
before I swallowed my soul back inside.

It grew like a child and made me nauseous
with truth. It got stuck
in my windpipe. The soul screamed.
I fought to swallow
the sound. Painkillers
did not work. The struggle
became louder. Finally
I looked for Grace to encourage
the soul's extension
into my hands, its descent
through my legs.

5

A canyon, a sister, a misfit monk
to cradle my ankles, a medicine woman
to press hard on my heart. Sandbags,
needles, pens. Queers
crips and beloved crazies
to listen and know. The experiments —
lovers reaching inside
and leaving, lovers holding
me down. Fists inside muscles, shaking
with what it might mean to stay.

One day a teacher to insist
I find the dignity in my spine
extend my quaking arms
toward something like a future
beside others extending theirs.
The soul filled out abandoned spaces.
The stories began burning
down into my feet, making light.
My steps began to hum.

Grace became a verb.

6

I carried my questions then
back to the sea and the patient desert. Still
they spoke of Grace. Grace, and storms.
Storms and justice.
Justice and the heartbeats
of our people. *Dreamers*
healers, rebels, you must walk
with your singing feet
toward the blood of sunrise
next to others grown full
from the walking.

Acknowledgements

So many people helped me over the years of living and writing that went into this book. I don't even know where to begin thanking you. But I'll try.

My deepest gratitude to my best friend and co-conspirator in dreams and revolution, Sascha Altman DuBrul. For sticking with me through the most brilliant and terrible of times. For teaching me about self-publishing the zines that led to this book. For unconditional love.

Gratitude to the poets whose books I read and re-read while crafting these poems. To Li-Young Lee, whose book *The City in Which I Love You* is "the volume of poetry that broke my voice open" mentioned in my poem "The Archaeology of Snow." To Yosef Komunyakaa, C.D. Wright, Joy Harjo, Khaled Mattawa, Matthea Harvey, Jericho Brown, and so many more great writers.

Many of these pieces were first drafted in the workshops offered by Jen Cross and Writing Ourselves Whole. Thanks for providing that nurturing, creative space, and thanks to all my workshop mates for your feedback and inspiration. To the San Francisco Queer Open Mic, whose events motivated me to get a new poem ready for performance every month, and where I found the space to explore queerness and gender in ways I'd never written about before. To the many performing poets who inspired me, particularly Meg Day and Sam Sax. To my writing buddy Liz Green. To Leah Lakshmi Piepzna-Samarasinha for her bad-assery, humor, solidarity, and careful readings of this manuscript. To Annah Anti-Palindrome, JDX, and everyone else at Deviant Type Press who offered me the opportunity to publish this book. To the teachers who believed in my writing way back when I was an isolated, obsessive teenager: Doctor Hollister, Hawley Rogers, Bruce Smith. To Anita Altman and Gil Kulick for sharing their home with Sascha and I so we could finish our books. To Anita for all the support she's given us with Icarus over the years.

So much gratitude to all the Icarus Project members with whom I've bared my soul, organized radical mental health events, put on artshows, toured across the world, co-written books and zines, and schemed up other outlandish visions and managed to pull them off. Particular thanks to my co-conspirators on the first (Inter)National Icarus Organizing Collective: Madigan Shive, Will Hall, Sascha DuBrul, and Carey Lamprecht.

To all the healers who've helped me through my journey, especially the folks in Generative Somatics.

To my given and chosen family – Gregory, Helen, Suzanne, Ella, Jamie, Petra, & Maru. Mom and Dad. To all my housemates over the years. To all my wild and beautiful friends who are out there making the world a more brilliant and just place: Marko, Leah, Liz, Beja, Kerb, Max, Kathy Rose, SB, George, Sarah Quinter, Sarah Hampton, Max Walsh, Kiran, Anthony Meza-Wilson, Gesine, Emiko, and so many more. To my comrades in somatics. To all the lovers and partners who appear in this book and who have transformed my life. To Ken Rosenthal for making the film Crooked Beauty and opening so many opportunities to me. To the Sick & Disabled Queers group, and to all the folks from whom I've been learning about disability justice. To all the people I have yet to know. May we cast our spells and change this mad mad world.

About the Author

Jacks McNamara is a genderqueer writer, artist, activist, and healer based in Santa Fe, New Mexico. Co-founder of The Icarus Project, an adventure in mutual aid & radical mental health support, and co-author of *Navigating the Space Between Brilliance and Madness,* Jacks has facilitated workshops and performed poetry across North America and Europe. Jacks was a 2012 Lambda Literary Fellow and has authored five zines, most recently, *So Many Ways to Be Beautiful.* A painter and designer, their creations have been shown across the US and Canada. Jacks is currently building a somatic healing practice, making everyone pancakes, geeking out on plant identification, and scheming about when they will get to raise goats in the country. Jacks' life and work are the subject of the documentary film *Crooked Beauty.*

Visit Jacks online at http://redwingedjacksbird.net.

About Deviant Type Press

We are an independent, radical, majority POC publishing collective. We are queers, working-class &/or poor artists, writers & zine-makers. We are school teachers and editors and parents and shit-starters who hate the white-supremacist, capitalist hetero-patriarchy. We are people who have a deep love for the art and writing created by our communities, and who think there should be more opportunities made for such gorgeous cultural work to be archived.

Deviant Type Press is dedicated to publishing transgressive, powerful literature written by queer, POC, and/or working class & poor artists. Our goal is to actively seek out and distribute poetry, creative non-fiction, lyric essays, graphic novels, zine collections, and fiction with non-traditional narratives (whether in form or content). We are particularly interested in genre-fucking/hybrid texts that obscure and challenge the borders between conventional literary categories.

As an independent press, we embrace the opportunity to publish first-time authors as well as writers who are interested in working closely with us through production, into distribution, and on towards public engagement and performance.

Simply put, our aim is to distribute literature that expresses the true complexity of being alive and the possibilities for personal and social change through literary art.